TRAIN YOUR BRAIN!
NUMBER PUZZLES

ARCTURUS

ARCTURUS

This edition published in 2024 by Arcturus Publishing Limited
26/27 Bickels Yard, 151–153 Bermondsey Street,
London SE1 3HA

Author: Lisa Regan
Illustrator: Evelyn Rogers
Designer: Amy McSimpson
Editor: Lydia Halliday
Managing Designers: Rosie Bellwood and Nathan Balsom
Managing Editor: Joe Harris

ISBN: 978-1-3988-3108-7
CH010838NT
Supplier 29, Date 0124, Print run 00004167

Printed in China

LET'S GET STARTED!

Are figures your forte and sums your superpower? Then you're in the right place! The puzzles in this book are all about the numbers, from zero to one thousand, and maybe even more!

Put your brain cells to the test, and see if you're a world class whizz when it comes to numbers. Prepare to be crowned king or queen of calculations!

Let's go!

Are you ready to start your puzzle journey? Each of the numbered clues on the right describes one of the pictures in the grid below. Write the correct number into the pink circles. Each row, column, and diagonal line of three squares adds up to 15.

1. This mode of transport has no engine.
2. Fly high in this one!
3. An everyday vehicle.
4. A two-wheeler powered by a person.
5. Take to the skies without wings.
6. You might see this one on safari.
7. Two wheels and lots of speed!
8. This one's handy for deliveries.
9. A no-nonsense work vehicle.

Seaside store

Cody and Callie are in California and can't wait to play on the beach. Who spent the most at the seaside store?

Give me five!

Complete this puzzle by writing a number from 1 to 5 into each square of this grid. Each row, column, and shape must contain all of those numbers, with no repetition.

Fun and games

Follow the arrows to help the clowns tumble and leap from the start to the finish. Move the number of spaces shown in the arrow each time.

START

FINISH

In the box

Solve the first problem, then copy your answer into the box indicated by the arrow.
Keep going, until you find the answer to the final equation.

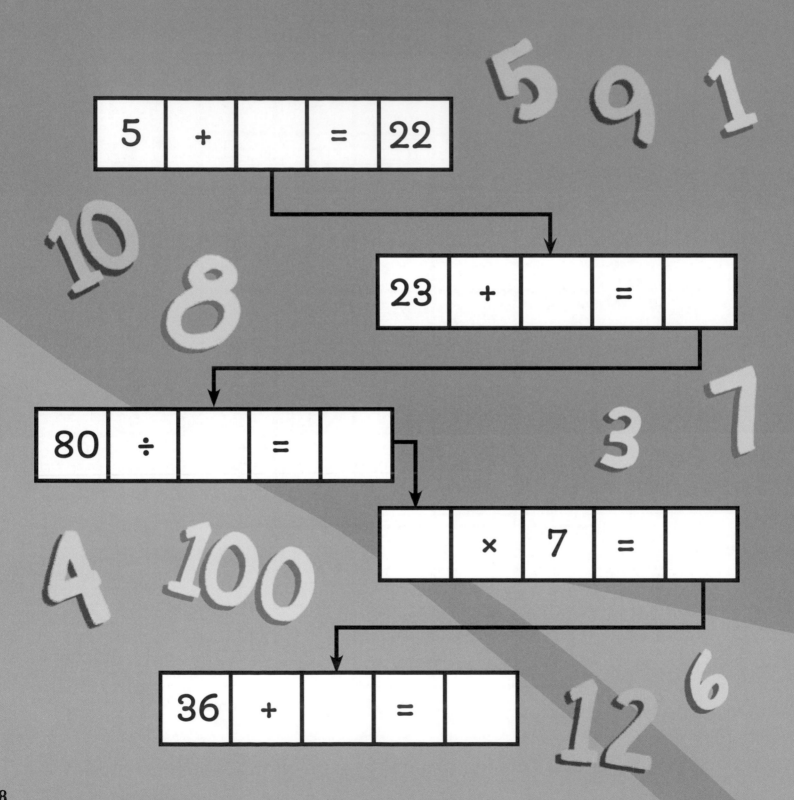

| 5 | + | | = | 22 |

| 23 | + | | = | |

| 80 | ÷ | | = | |

| | × | 7 | = | |

| 36 | + | | = | |

Making tracks

Draw lines to complete this grid. Each square of the grid should have a single diagonal line. The numbers tell you how many diagonal lines meet at that point; for example, a 0 has no diagonals touching it, while a 2 has 2 diagonals touching it.

Some lines have been added to start the puzzle.

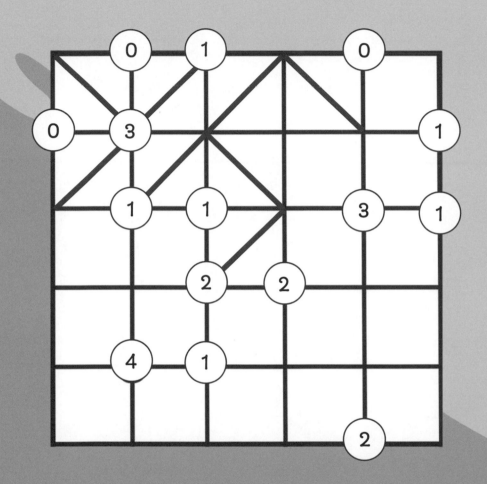

Dinosaur herder

The green dinosaurs should be in two groups of four, and the brown dinosaurs should be in two groups of four. If you swap a green dinosaur directly with an brown dinosaur, what's the lowest number of swaps for you to put them into their correct groups?

party prices

How much has Molly Mayhew spent online at the party store?

$0.08

$1.10

$0.20

$0.75

$0.99

$1.25

NUMBER OF ITEMS IN CART

10

8

7

5

8

7

11

On thin ice

Which of these polar bears can reach the mainland without sinking? Each bear must step on every piece of ice in their lane. Pieces of ice marked with numbers that are multiples of seven are safe.

MAINLAND

Island gardens

Divide this island into L-shaped gardens. Each garden must contain the numbers 1, 2, 3, and 4. You must use every square, with no numbers left. The L-shapes can be rotated or flipped and two have been done for you.

3	1	2	2	3	4	2	3
4	1	4	3	4	1	2	1
1	3	2	2	1	3	4	1
4	4	1	4	2	4	4	2
1	2	2	3	1	3	2	3
3	4	3	1	2	3	1	1
4	3	1	3	2	3	4	3
1	2	4	1	2	4	4	2

Castle defenders

Fill the empty squares in the grid, so that there are the numbers 1 to 9 in every number in each row, column, and mini-grid of nine squares.

8		1	6				9	4
		6	2	8		1		3
		7				6		5
7	2		4	9			3	
4			8	3	2			7
	9			7	1		2	8
3		9				7		
5		4		2	3	8		
1	8				5	3		9

Join the dots

Draw lines between all of the dots, following the rules below.

- Lines can't cross each other or form a T-junction.
- You must go through a white circle in straight line.
- You must change direction when you go through a black circle.
- You can either change direction or go straight through a dot with no circle.

Some lines have been added to start the puzzle.

Target practice

Take aim ... and score! Which of the archers has scored the most in this competition?

Guitar heroes

Match each guitar to its owner by solving the equations.

A 21 + 29

B 4 × 12

C 7 × 7

D 92 ÷ 2

E 76 − 29

46

47

48

49

50

Keep the change!

Four diners ate at a New York restaurant and they each paid for their meal with a $100 bill. These trays show the change given to each diner. Work out how much each meal cost.

Change: $23.18

Change: $19.76

Change: $20.02

Change: $14.54

Lock and key

Which key will unlock the treasure chest? Solve the equations to work it out.

5 × 8

48

4 × 11

94 ÷ 2

6 × 7

8 × 6

85 − 39

9 × 4

Ancient games

The Romans loved to play dice games. Use the numbers from all three visible faces of these dice (reading from left to right) to work out the totals. The first one has been done for you.

264 + 654 = 918

Camel travel

Guide this camel through the desert to reach the oasis.
It may step only on hexagons that are divisible by four.

FINISH

START

Show how you feel

Work out the number value of each emoji in the grid.
The numbers outside the grid are the sum of each row or column.
One has been found for you.

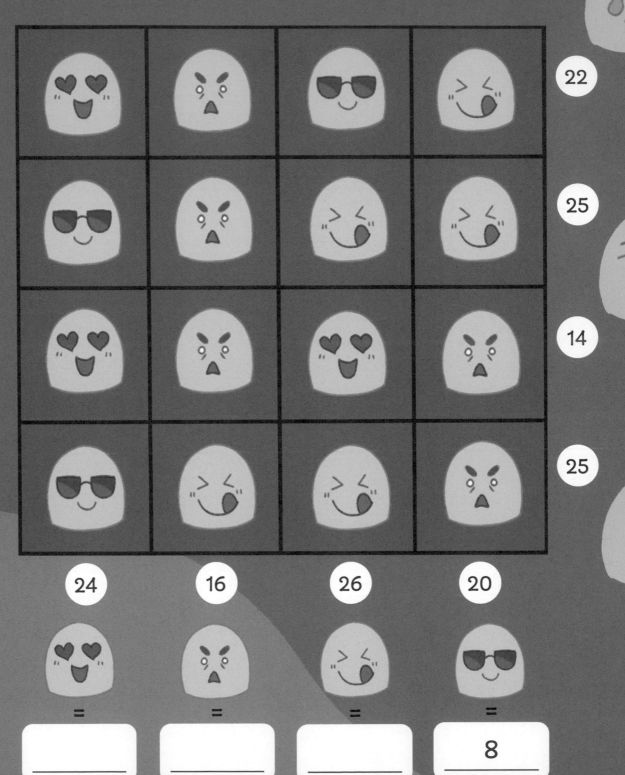

Seeing stars

Fill the grid with the numbers 1 to 4. Each row and column can contain only one of each number. A white star tells you that the two squares on either side of the star have consecutive numbers (eg 2, 3). If there is no star, the numbers are NOT consecutive.

Thirsty work

Three baristas each made four types of drink. Add the numbers on each type of drink to work out total number sold. Which drink was most popular?

Espresso

Tea

Milkshake

Coffee

10

16

31

23

35

19

46

28

50

14

49

37

Answer =

Under the sea

Can you place the five different sea creatures into the grid so that every row and column contains only one of each?

Magic souvenirs

Willow Witch had fun at the Wizwarts theme park and now wants to spend her gold coins on some souvenirs.

1. Willow wants to buy a pair of earrings, a necklace, and a cap. How much does she need?

PENCILS - 1 coin

KEYRINGS - 2 coins

NECKLACE - 4 coins

BOOK - 7 coins

EARRINGS - 4 coins

CHOCOLATE BROOMSTICK - 1 coin

CRYSTAL BALL - 10 coins

CAP - 5 coins

2. If she has 10 coins and buys keyrings for three friends, will she have enough for a spell book?

3. If she has 10 coins and buys a necklace, how many chocolate broomsticks can she buy?

4. Which costs more: four pairs of earrings or a crystal ball and a cap?

Seal Spotting

A group of seals are lurking under the ice. Can you find them? The numbers show how many seals are in the squares touching (up, down, across, or diagonally). Draw an "X" where the seals appear. One has been done for you.

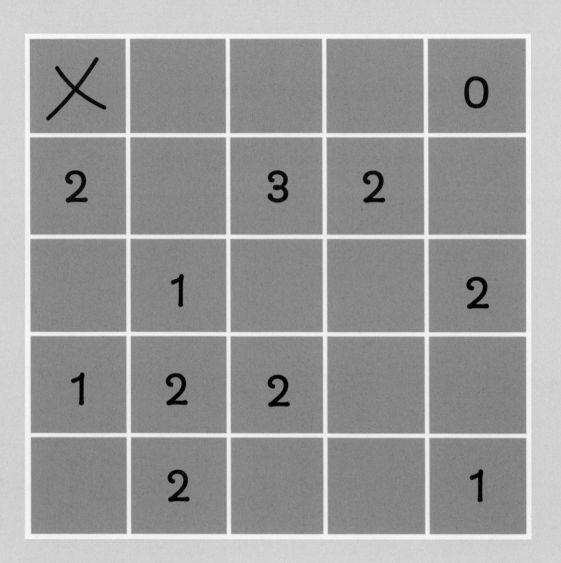

Heavy hippos

Which of these happy hippos weighs the most? Work out the calculations on each to find out.

A. ½ of 9

B. 8 – 3.8

C. 2.2 × 2

D. 16 ÷ 4

E. 2.7 + 1.9

F. 6.3 – 2.2

G. 8.6 ÷ 2

On the slopes

Harvey and Hazel skied down the mountain four times each. Here are their times. Can you answer the questions below?

	First run	Second run	Third run	Fourth run
Harvey	3 minutes, 20 seconds	2 minutes, 40 seconds	2 minutes, 45 seconds	3 minutes, 15 seconds
Hazel	2 minutes, 55 seconds	3 minutes, 10 seconds	3 minutes, 55 seconds	3 minutes, 10 seconds

1. Who recorded the fastest time for one run?

2. Adding up all the runs, who was fastest overall?

3. What was Harvey's average time? To find out, divide Harvey's total time by the number of runs.

Making music

Make some noise! Work out the answers to the problems using the number code.

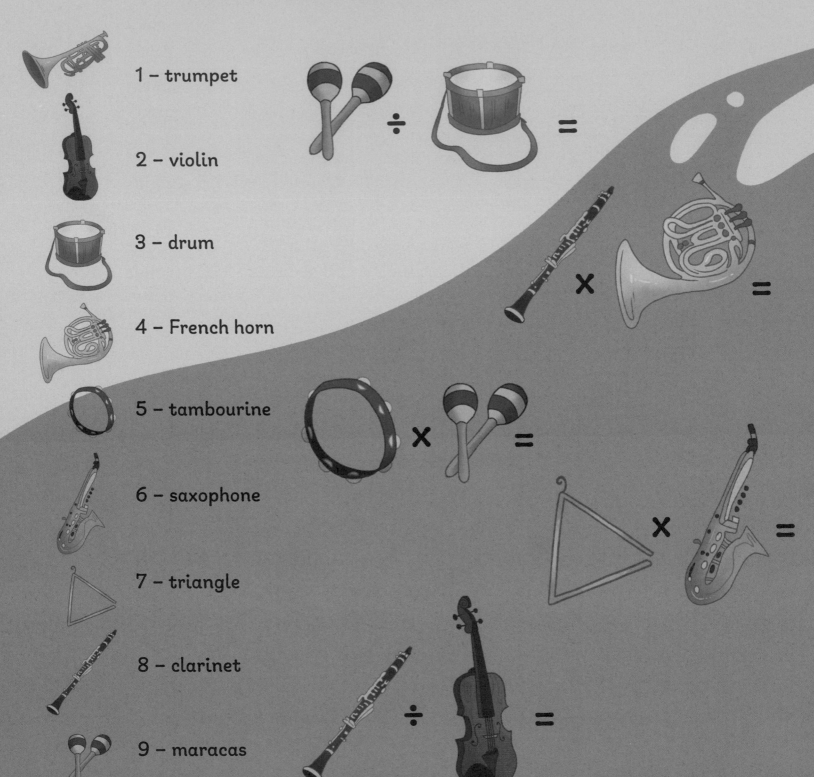

1 – trumpet

2 – violin

3 – drum

4 – French horn

5 – tambourine

6 – saxophone

7 – triangle

8 – clarinet

9 – maracas

Under the sea

Draw straight lines to connect each pair of matching numbers. A line cannot cross another line, or pass through a square that already contains a line. The first line has been done for you.

pirate pyramid

Fill in the numbers on the pile of cannonballs. Each one is the sum of the two cannonballs below it, like the example in the middle of the bottom row (1 + 1 = 2).

Black and white

The pandas have laid out their bamboo sticks in this pattern. What is the biggest three digit number you can make by moving two sticks?

Modern art

Can you find each of the three blocks in this bold, bright piece of artwork?

4	8	9	3	4	5	1	7
5	1	3	5	9	1	2	5
7	6	2	8	4	5	8	3
4	2	9	6	3	7	6	1
3	6	4	1	6	2	4	7
8	1	7	3	9	7	3	9
1	8	9	8	5	4	5	2
9	4	5	1	2	2	7	6

1	7
8	9

2	4
7	3

2	8
9	6

All adrift

The astronaut has lost her bearings and can't find a way back to the rocket.
Which of the arrows eventually leads to where she wants to go?
Move the number of spaces shown on each arrow, in the direction it is pointing.

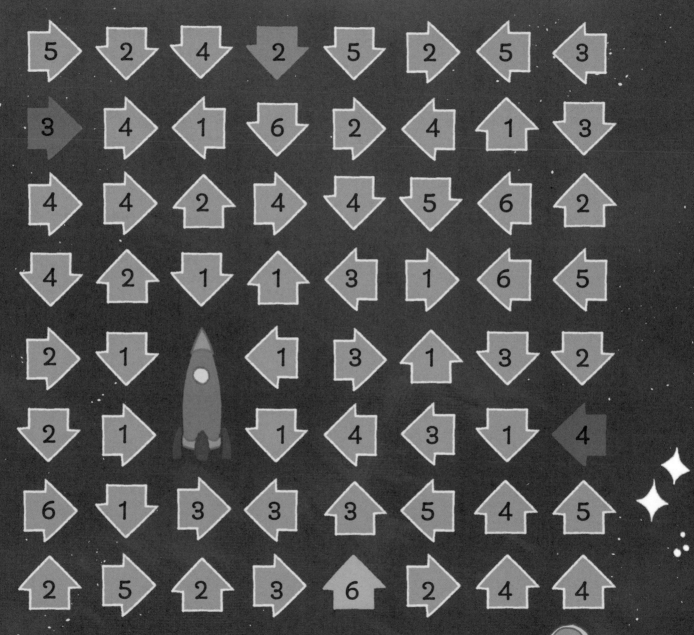

Baker's dozen

Circle the donuts or pastries that are multiples of 12. The letters will spell the name of the baker's best-selling cake.

144 R

24 E

60 D

96 V

80 A

74 N

48 E

66 I

120 L

72 V

42 U

18 C

106 O

108 E

68 G

36 T

Letter mystery

Can you work out which letter is missing from each of the yellow sections? Each letter represents its number in the alphabet.

To help you, fill in this grid showing the position of each letter in the alphabet.

A	B	C	D	E	F	G	H	I	J	K	L	M
1	2	3										

N	O	P	Q	R	S	T	U	V	W	X	Y	Z

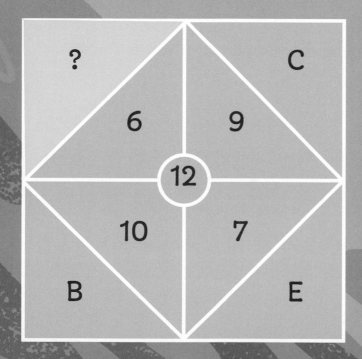

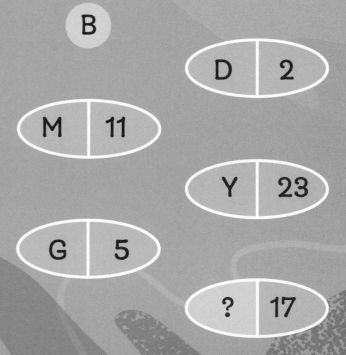

Hideaway

Guide this aardvark through its burrow to its babies, adding up the numbers as you go. What is the total of its route?

START

10

4   15

8

7

16

3

2

2   9

14

6

20

5

11   13

FINISH

It all adds up

Shade some of the squares so that they add up to the totals (shown in large numbers) on the end of columns and rows.

The squares have the value of the small numbers so the first square on a row or column is 1 and the second square is 2.

Example

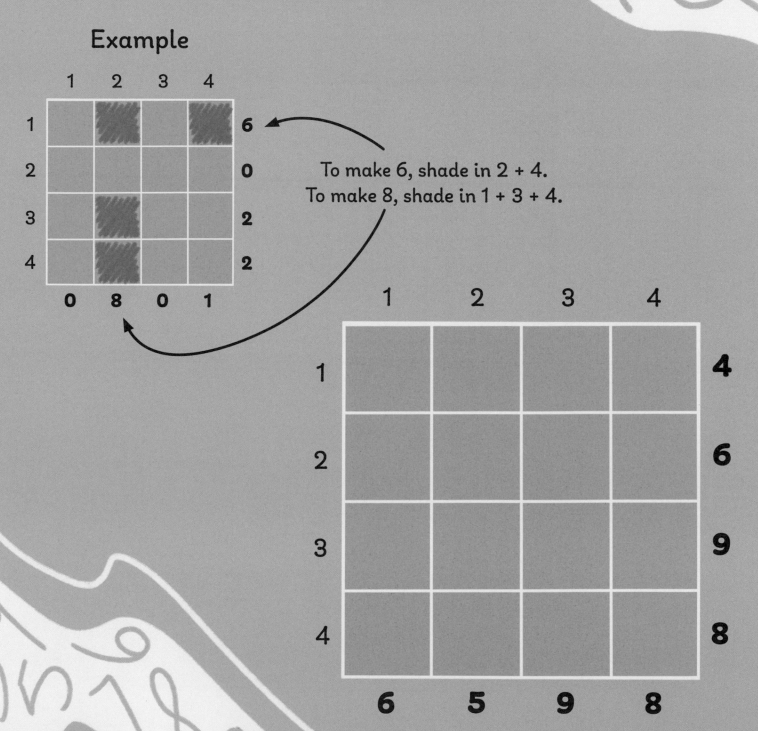

To make 6, shade in 2 + 4.
To make 8, shade in 1 + 3 + 4.

Whack-a-mole

Where are the moles going to pop up? The numbered squares tell you how many moles are in the squares touching them (up, down, across, or diagonally). One mole has been found for you, but see if you can locate them all!

pirate games

Work out the calculations on the skull dice, working from left to right for each one. Which pirate has the highest score?

Night Sky

Can you cross out one digit in each equation to make it correct? For example, 2 + 13 = 5 is wrong, but it can be made right by crossing out the "1", leaving 2 + 3 = 5.

$$28 + 19 = 27$$

$$437 - 22 = 25$$

$$2 \times 612 = 24$$

$$36 \div 6 = 63$$

Toil and trouble

The numbers rising in the steam from the witch's brew are part of a sequence.
Put them in order and work out which number is missing.

28

21

56

49

14

84

63

42

35

7

77

Race to the finish

Find a path through the race cars to the finish flag. You must move from car to car in this order: 1, 2, 3, 4, then back to 1. You must also follow this pattern: red, yellow, green, then back to red.

Beautiful butterflies

Each of these flowers has a butterfly in a square directly next to it. Can you find all the hidden butterflies by using these clues? One has already been found for you.

Each butterfly is above, below, or to the side of its flower.

No butterfly is in a square touching another butterfly, not even diagonally.

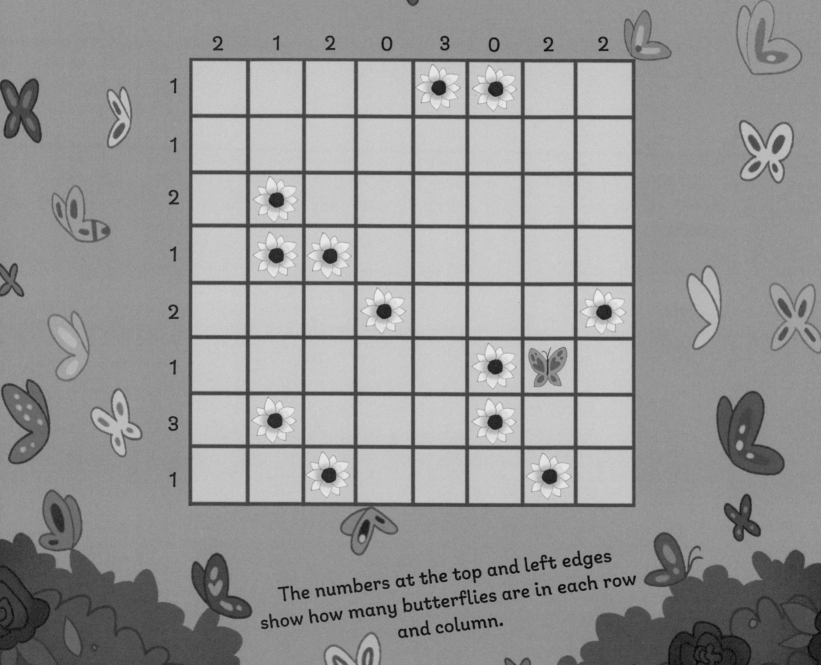

The numbers at the top and left edges show how many butterflies are in each row and column.

Pet puzzlers

Complete these puzzles by placing the numbers into the jigsaw shapes. Each row, column, and shape must contain the numbers 1 to 5, with no repetition.

Minibeasts

How well do you know your bugs and beasties? Each of the numbered clues on the right describes one of the pictures in the grid below. Write the correct number into the yellow circles.

Hint: each row, column, and diagonal line of three squares adds up to 15.

1. Fly away home, dotty creature!
2. This insect is a master of the high jump.
3. A winged wonder that begins life as a crawler.
4. It lives in a colony with its fellow workers.
5. A creature that carries its home with it.
6. An eight-legged spinning machine.
7. This striped insect is a flower's friend.
8. More legs than most!
9. An aerial acrobat with shimmering shades.

Turtle travel

Sea turtles can cover hundreds or even thousands of miles when they migrate. Add up the numbers on each turtle's route to find out which one has swum the farthest.

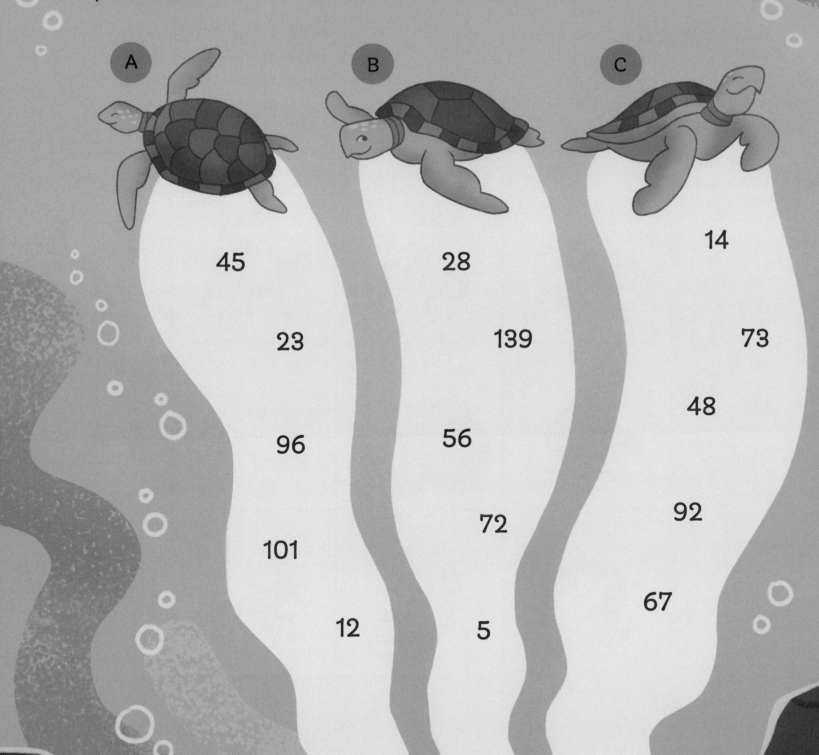

A

45

23

96

101

12

B

28

139

56

72

5

C

14

73

48

92

67

Unicorn match

Which of these unicorns belong to the same herd? Find the two unicorns whose numbers add up to the same total.

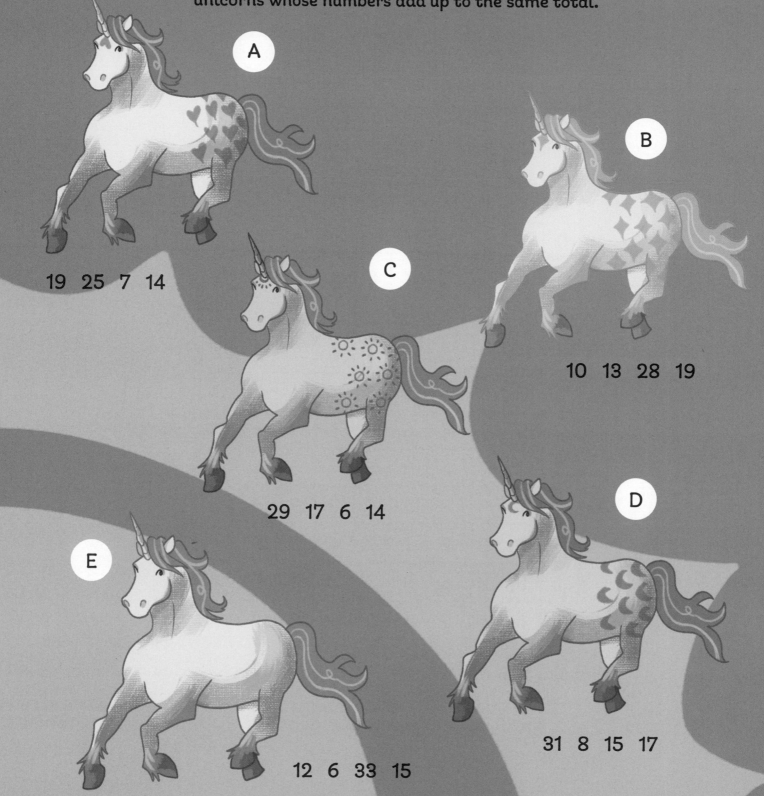

A

B

C

19 25 7 14

10 13 28 19

29 17 6 14

D

E

31 8 15 17

12 6 33 15

Call me!

Can you find the six-digit telephone number hidden just once in the grid? It could appear sideways or up and down, but not diagonally.

569821

4	7	5	8	1	5	2	3	7	2
2	4	1	2	9	6	2	6	1	9
1	5	6	9	1	9	4	9	3	7
7	1	6	3	5	8	1	5	4	3
9	2	5	6	1	6	2	6	4	6
8	6	2	5	7	3	5	9	8	2
2	4	8	4	3	2	9	8	2	1
1	5	3	6	9	9	6	2	1	7
3	7	9	3	5	8	4	1	5	8
2	9	7	4	6	8	2	8	3	8
5	1	7	5	9	5	7	6	1	4
9	7	6	8	5	1	3	9	6	1
5	6	9	8	2	7	4	9	8	7
1	3	8	6	9	5	8	1	6	2
9	6	2	7	4	2	9	8	2	1

Can you also find a block of 4 that has two pairs of numbers, diagonally opposite each other—like this (but not necessarily 2 and 4):

2 4
4 2

City Scene

Fill each empty square with a number from 1 to 6, following these rules.

- No number may appear twice in any horizontal row or vertical column.
- In any set of two squares separated by dotted lines, one square contains an odd number and the other square contains an even number.

	2	6			5
			3		
	5	1	2		6
			5		1
	6		4		
2		5		1	3

Compass calculations

Each of the compass points (North, South, East, and West) represents a mathematical symbol (+ − x ÷). Work out which is which so that these equations work properly, both across and down.

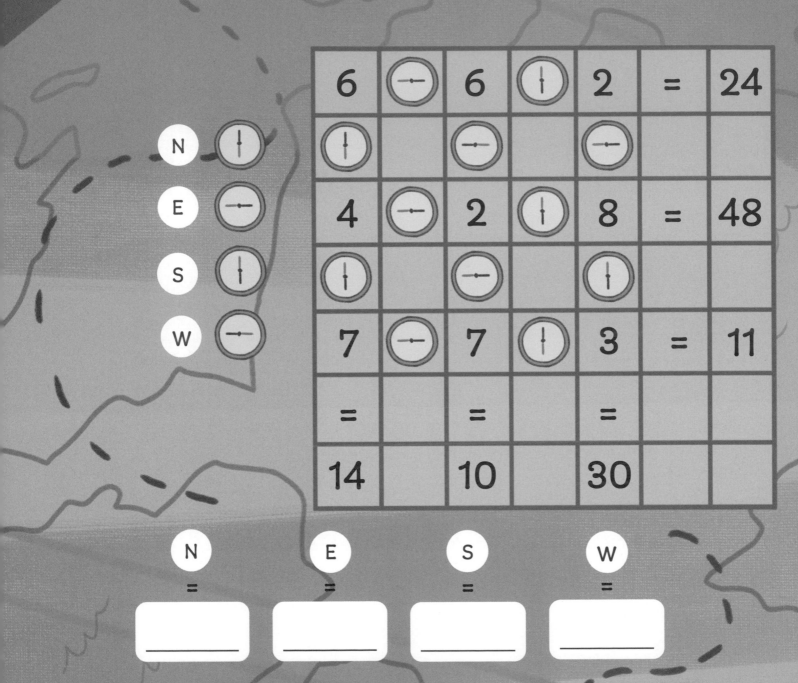

N =

E =

S =

W =

Loop the loop

Here's a graph showing the number of people that rode the roller coaster over a week. Can you answer the questions below?

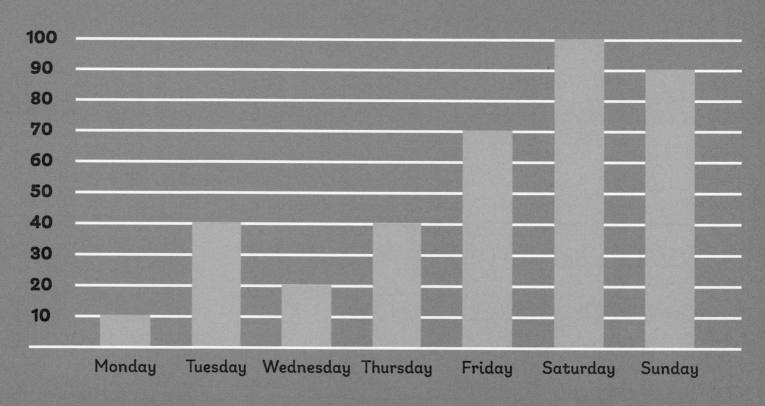

1. What days had the same number of riders?

2. Were there more riders in total on weekdays or the weekend?

3. If each rider paid €1.50, how much money did the roller coaster take on Thursday?

4. How many more visitors were there on Saturday than Tuesday?

That's torn it!

These two crazy kitties have made a mess. Match the torn scraps of paper into pairs, each with an equal equation. One has been done for you.

7×5 = $49 - 14$

$54 - 9$

21×2

0.5×66

5×5

$17 + 18$

0.5×70

6×7

3×11

$100 \div 4$

15×3

Fast food

Work out the number that each food or drink item represents. The numbers at the ends of the rows and columns are the sum of all four items. No item represents a number higher than 8.

City lights

Place the four circled numbers into the grid so that the calculations from top to bottom and left to right are correct.

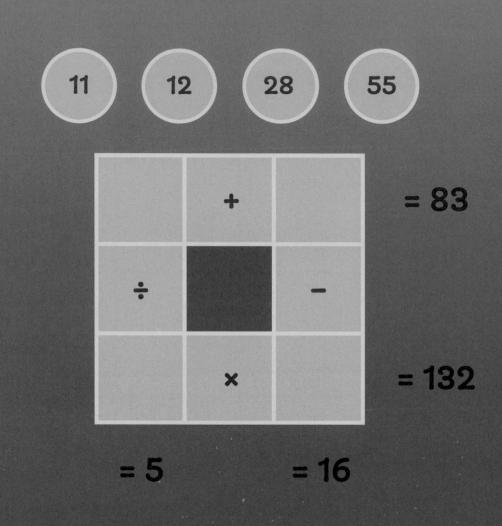

(11)   (12)   (28)   (55)

Grid:

	+		= 83
÷	■	−	
	×		= 132

= 5   = 16

Birthday brain teasers

Happy birthday to Tara! See if you can work out Tara's and Bruno's ages in these riddles.

When Tara was 6, her sister Amy was half her age. If Tara is 15 today, how old is Amy?

When Tara's brother, Bruno, was 15, their dad was 37. Now, their dad is twice Bruno's age. How old is Bruno?

Safe and sound

Eric has asked Johannes to collect his bike for him. He has sent the code as four separate problems. What numbers should Johannes use to unlock the bike?

1. (8 × 9) ÷ 12

2. 1 ÷ 0.5

3. (100 − 51) ÷ 7

4. 81 ÷ 9

1.

2.

3.

4.

Letters and numbers

Can you work out which letter is missing from each of the pink sections?
Each letter represents its number in the alphabet.

A	B	C	D	E	F	G	H	I	J	K	L	M
1	2	3										

N	O	P	Q	R	S	T	U	V	W	X	Y	Z

To help you, fill in this grid showing the position of each letter in the alphabet.

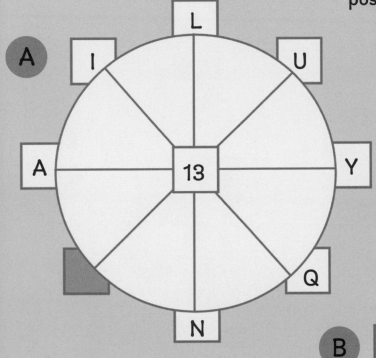

A

L I U A 13 Y Q N

B

10	8	4	3
6	3	1	3
5	6	3	1
5	3	5	5
Z	T	M	

Get outta here

Which cowboy has ridden the farthest out of town? Add up the numbers on each of their hoof trails to find out.

A
43
76
29
18
60

B
15
82
47
36
51

C
64
17
55
38
29

Calculation totals

Shade some of the squares so that they add up to the totals (shown in large numbers) on the end of columns and rows.

The squares have the value of the small numbers so the first square on a row or column is 1 and the second square is 2.

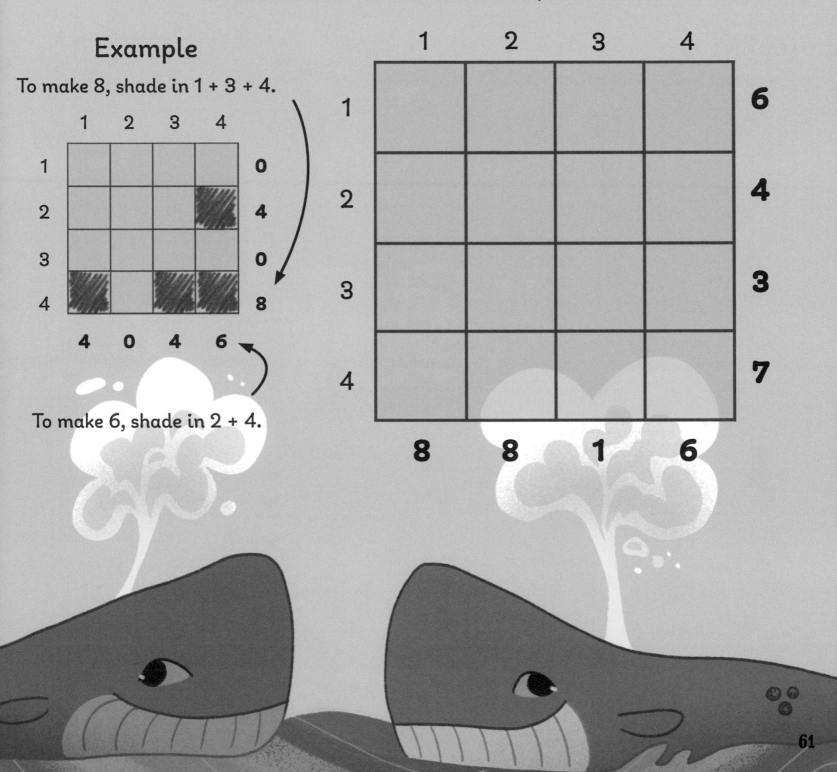

Example

To make 8, shade in 1 + 3 + 4.

	1	2	3	4	
1					0
2				▨	4
3					0
4	▨		▨	▨	8
	4	0	4	6	

To make 6, shade in 2 + 4.

	1	2	3	4	
1					6
2					4
3					3
4					7
	8	8	1	6	

Cow counting

How many brown patches should you draw on the central cow?
Use the number of patches on the others to work it out.

Lost and found

These squirrels have buried all their acorns and need to find them again. The numbered squares tell you how many acorns are in the squares touching them (up, down, across, or diagonally). Draw the acorns into the squares where they should appear.

		1		1
1				
2	2			2
	2		2	1

On the run

Which of the bobsleigh teams finished first? And what position did each of the other bobsleigh teams finish?

The red team didn't come in the top three.

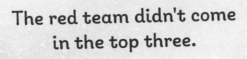

A team with yellow helmets finished second.

The green striped bobsleigh finished ahead of both teams wearing yellow helmets.

The team with a flame logo wasn't last.

The blue bobsleigh beat three other teams.

The ones wearing turquoise helmets finished one place ahead of the red team and one place behind the team with the yellow bobsleigh.

The hats have it

Work out what number is represented by each of the hats. The numbers at the end of each row and column is the sum of all four items. One has been found for you.

Hint: only one of the types of hats equals an even number.

Bright lights, big city

Which of the times tables is represented by each skyscraper? Write it in the space at the bottom, and then fill in the missing numbers in the windows.

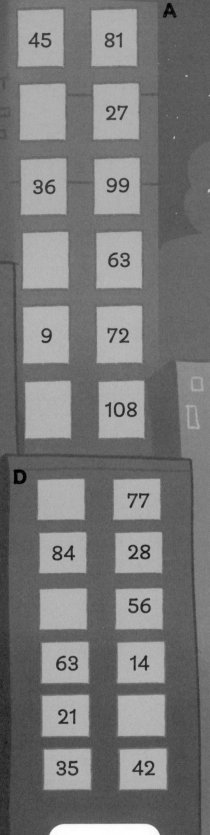

A

45	81
	27
36	99
	63
9	72
	108

C

32	44
	8
12	36
16	20
	28
48	

_____

B

44	
77	132
	22
121	66
110	33
	88

_____

D

	77
84	28
	56
63	14
21	
35	42

_____

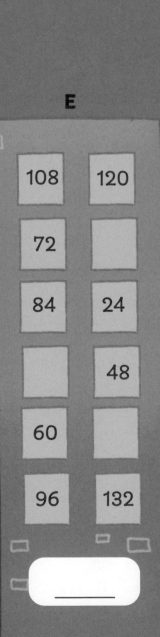

E

108	120
72	
84	24
	48
60	
96	132

_____

Star Struck

Fill the grids with the numbers 1 to 4. Each row and column can contain only one of each number. A star tells you that the two squares each side have consecutive numbers (eg 3, 4). If there is no star, the numbers are NOT consecutive.

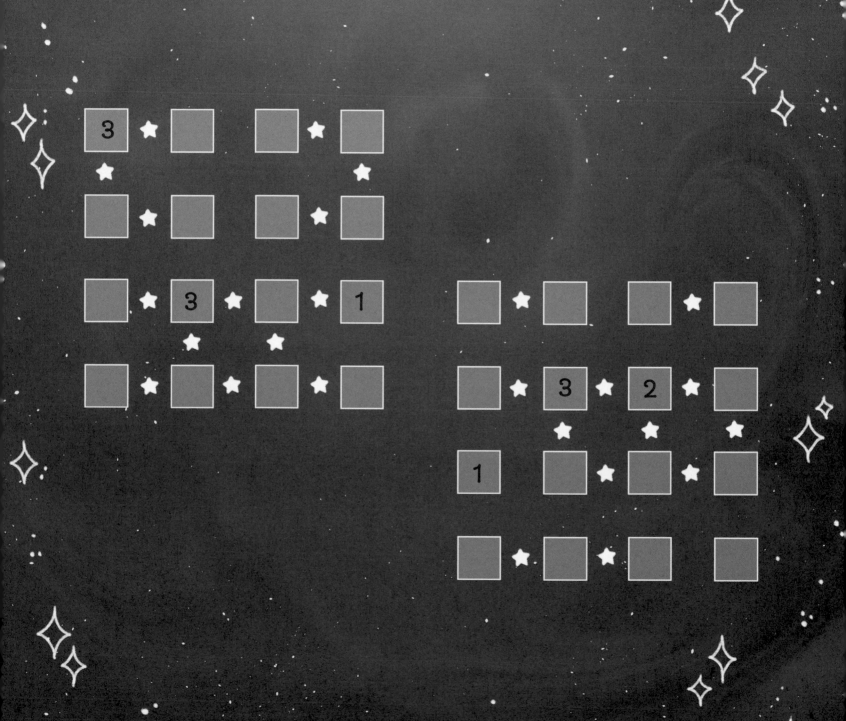

START

Splat attack

Find a path going top to bottom from splat to splat, using only calculations that have an even number as an answer.

8 × 4

67 – 12

54 ÷ 9

5 × 6

42 ÷ 6

11 × 3

0.5 × 74

19 + 64

102 ÷ 2

3 × 7

8 × 9

7 × 7

12 × 9

12 × 12

47 + 35

15 × 4

FINISH

35 ÷ 7

68

Let me in

Can you find out Nate's four-digit passcode? Work out the answer to each calculation, then cross them off in the grid. The answers appear reading left to right or top to bottom. The numbers that are left are the passcode.

117 x 5 =

481 – 18 =

1463 + 20 =

8 x 7 =

842 ÷ 2 =

11 x 11 =

754 – 628 =

150 x 12 =

7 x 12 =

6 x 12 =

6 x 7 =

81 ÷ 3 =

121 x 3 =

Write it right

Help Jesse work out which number is larger. Circle the larger number on each line.

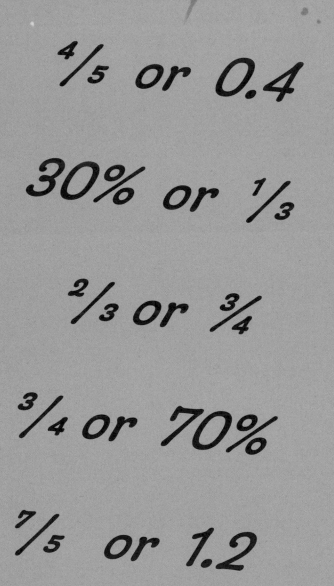

⁴/₅ or 0.4

30% or ¹/₃

²/₃ or ³/₄

³/₄ or 70%

⁷/₅ or 1.2

Lost in space

Which is the alien's home planet?
Solve these problems to find out.

1. The planet does not have any repeated numbers.

2. It is not an odd number.

3. The planet does not have a number that is a multiple of 5.

4. The number is below 8 x 12.

5. The number is above 9 x 9.

88

78

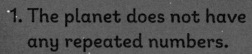

98

95

94

90

87

Pirate puzzlers

Complete these puzzles by placing numbers into the jigsaw shapes. Each row, column, and shape must contain the numbers 1 to 5, with no repetition.

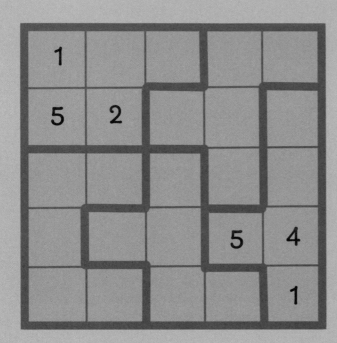

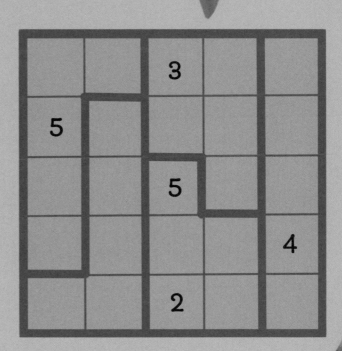

Gimme five

Divide the grid into five sets of five, so that each set contains the numbers 1 to 5. A set can be connected sideways or up and down, but not diagonally. The first set has been done for you.

3	2	3	5	4
2	4	1	4	1
5	2	4	2	5
3	5	1	3	1
5	1	3	4	2

The chosen one

Which cake is Harriet going to buy? Follow the clues to find out which treat is left when you have eliminated the others.

Cross out any number divisible by 6.

Cross out multiples of 4.

Cross out factors of 15.

Cross out numbers in the 7 times table.

3

5

12

18

22

8

14

21

24

20

28

30

Bold and beautiful

Which of the beautiful butterflies has numbers that add up to exactly 50?

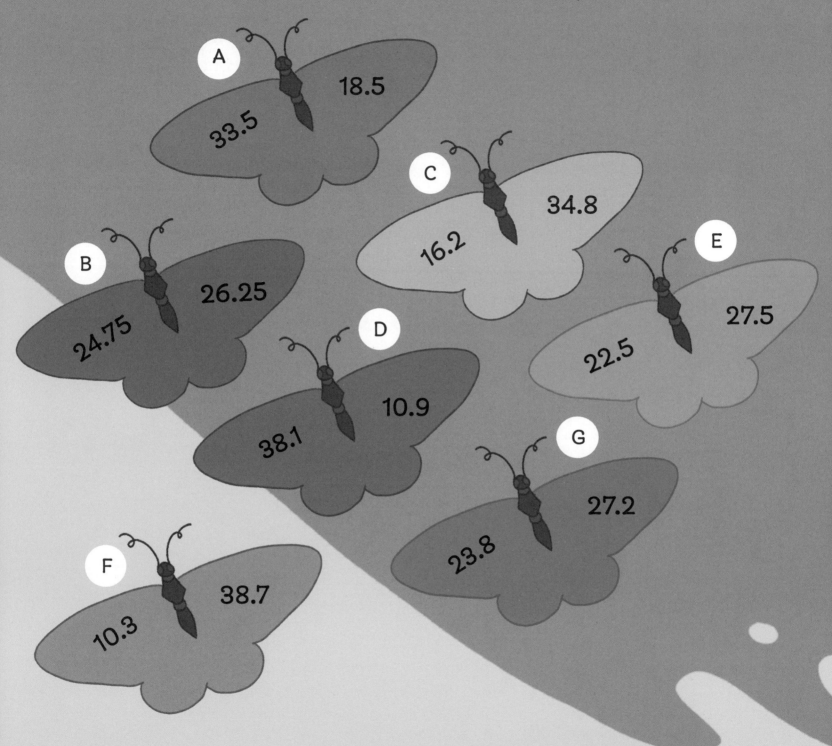

Food for thought

The grapes and bananas in each line form a sequence.
Can you complete the pattern by adding to the final,
single fruit each time to make the correct number?

Strike one!

Each baseball item has a different value. The total for each row and column is shown at the side and underneath the grid. Can you work out what each item is worth? The ball has been done for you.

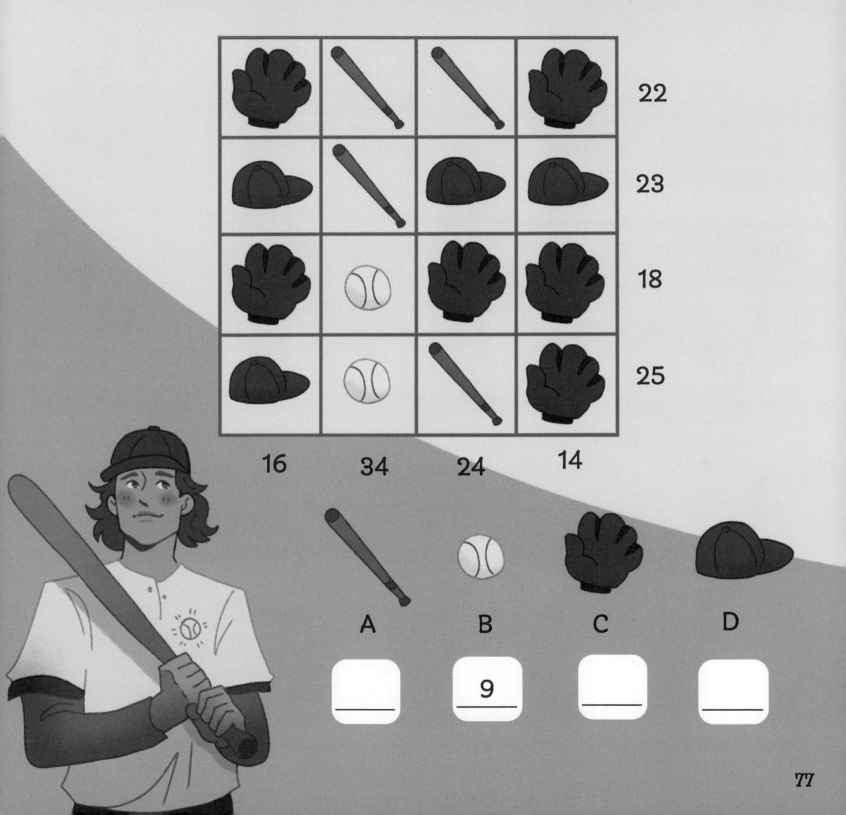

A ___

B _9_

C ___

D ___

Burger bar

Which of these burgers are from the seven times table?
Can you spot anything else they have in common?

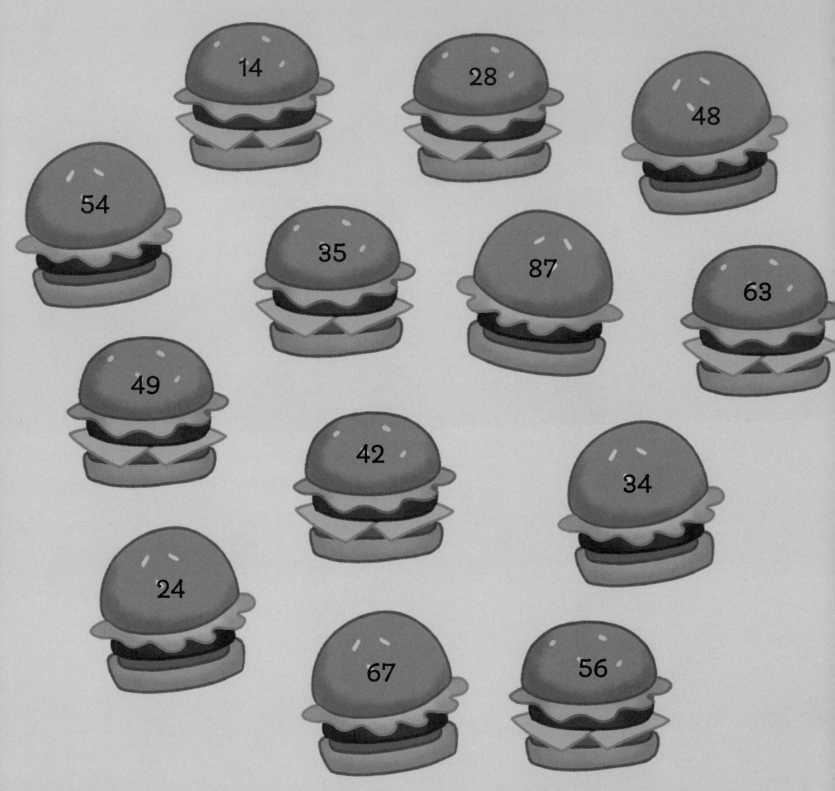

Beach brainbox

Match up each shell with a starfish so the paired numbers add up to 48.

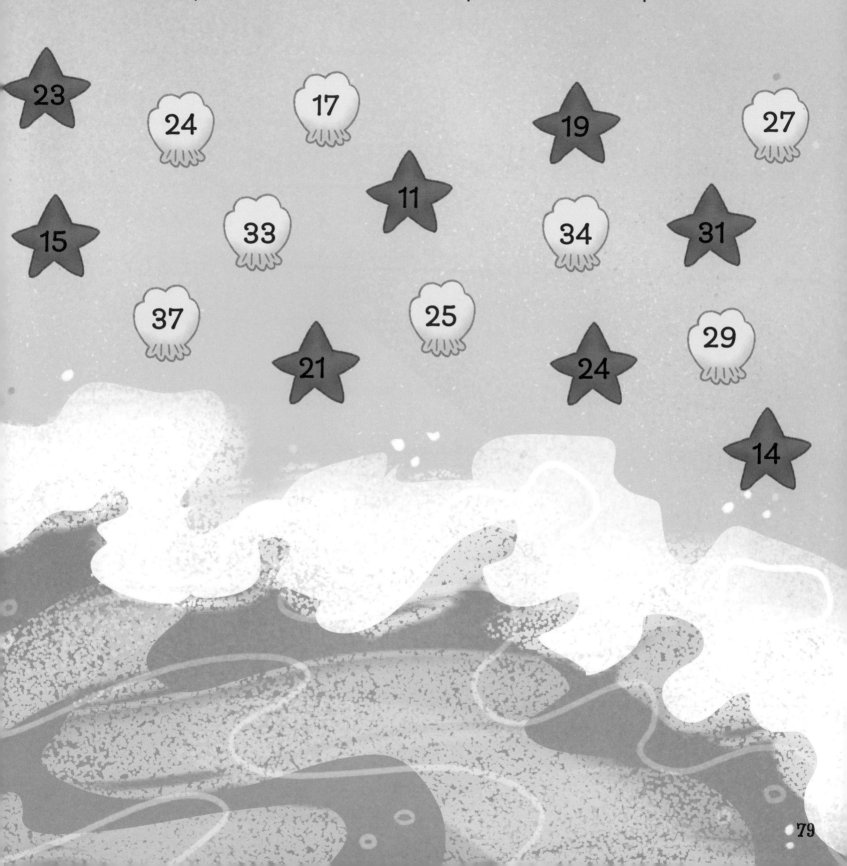

Two for one

If you like sudoku puzzles, you'll love this double puzzle! The central shaded area is the bottom of the top grid, and the top of the bottom grid.

Solve it as two separate puzzles, following the usual rules: each row, column and mini-grid must contain the numbers from 1 to 6 just once.

	3				1
			2		
4			5	6	2
5	2		1		
	4				
1				3	
	3		4		
2	6		3	1	

Australian animals

Each of these Aussie animals has been given a value.
Work out which group adds up to the largest total.

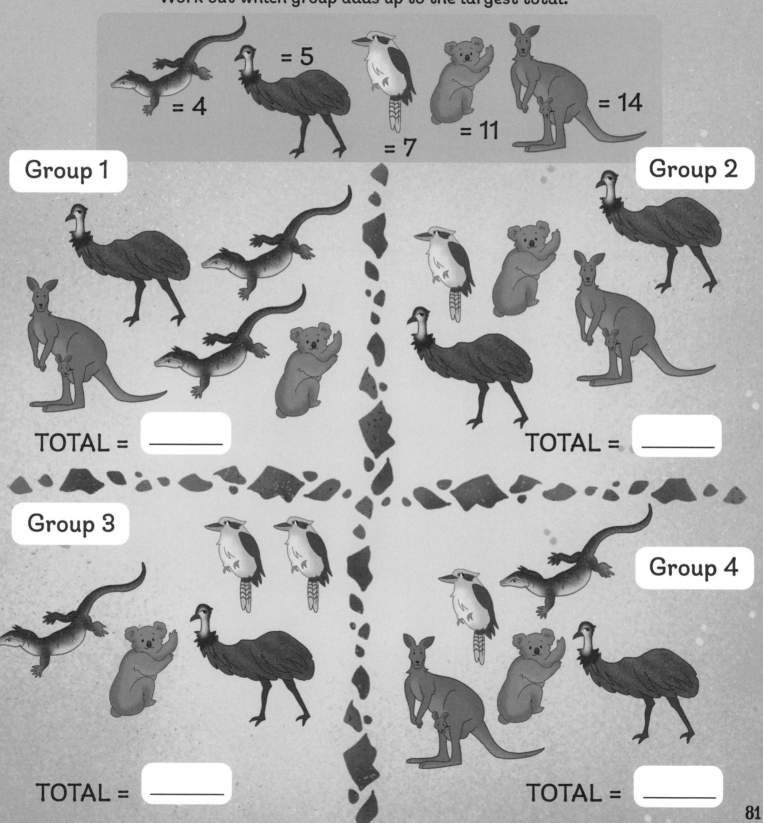

= 4

= 5

= 7

= 11

= 14

Group 1

TOTAL = _____

Group 2

TOTAL = _____

Group 3

TOTAL = _____

Group 4

TOTAL = _____

Dot to dot

Make one, continuous line around this grid following these rules.

1. Dots can be joined with horizontal and vertical lines, but not diagonals.
2. Each number indicates how many lines surround it.
3. Not all dots have to be joined.

Some lines are there for you already.

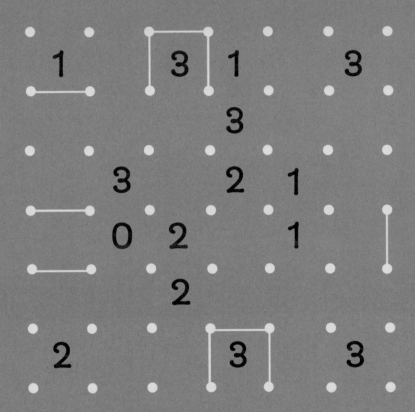

Setting Sail

Follow the path of each boat to see which has numbers adding up to the SMALLEST total.

A

B

10

33

4

51

17

6

18

17

20

41

27

25

8

16

5

29

46

14

C

11

8

D

Eggs-actly!

Find all of the eggs that are factors of 100 and use them
to spell another way of serving eggs to eat.

Perfect fit

Which of the key stones will drop exactly into place to finish the arch? The calculation on it needs to equal 64.

7 × 8   132 ÷ 2   37 + 29   95 − 21   13 × 5   77 − 13   33 × 2

Tug of war

Which of the scraps of paper match up to make equal pairs,
like the one the chipmunks have just torn in two?

11 × 4

17 × 2

54 × 0.5

30 ÷ 2

6 × 3 = 36 ÷ 2

18 + 16

59 – 15

60 – 17

25 + 18

45 ÷ 3

3 × 9

Tent totals

A tent is only waterproof if its numbers add up to exactly 99.
Which campers are going to get wet?

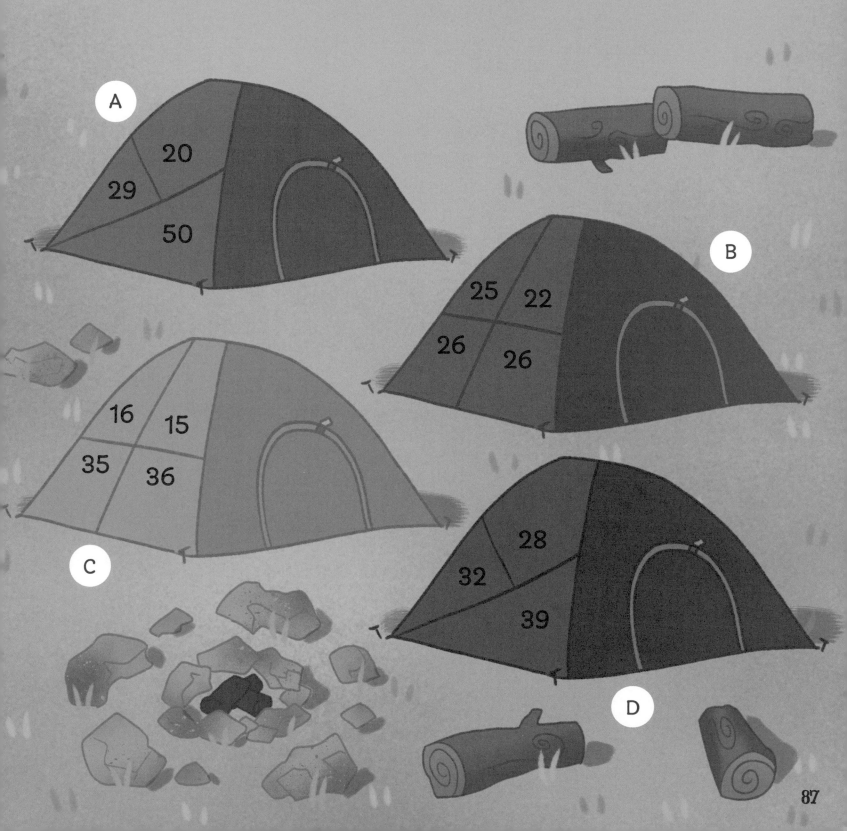

A 20 29 50

B 25 22 26 26

C 16 15 35 36

D 28 32 39

On the hop

Each frog hops from one numbered lily pad to the next, until it reaches a flower.
If you add up the numbers on the lily pads, which frog has the highest total?

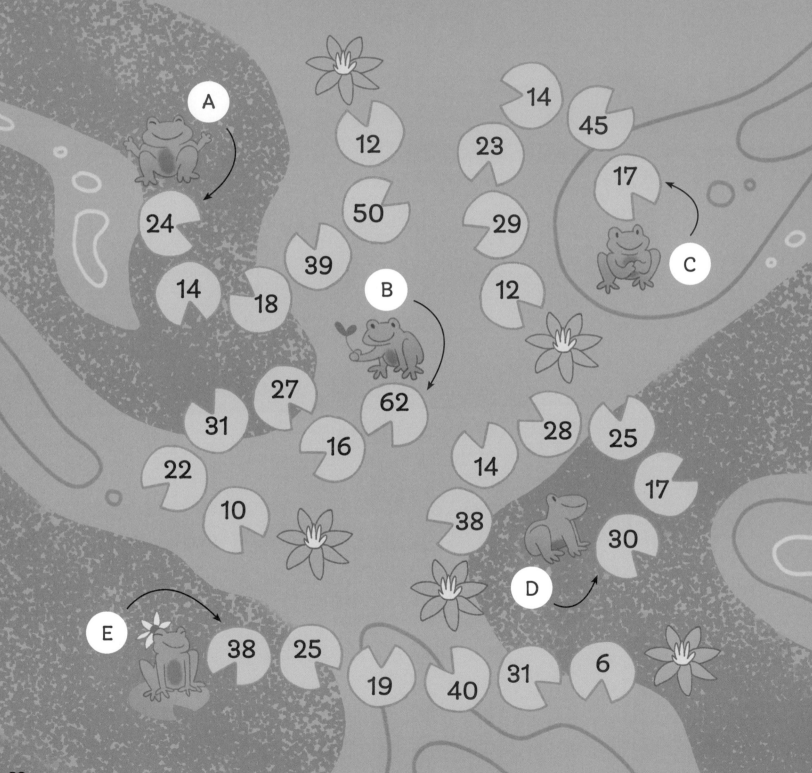

Bug pile

Fill in the numbers on the circles. Each one is the sum of the two circles below it. Work your way up to the top of the pile and find the final total.

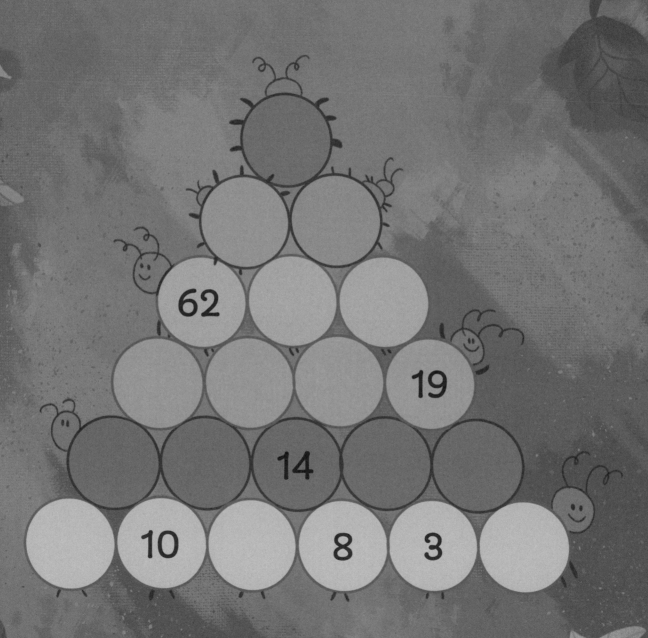

Cafe Culture

The total for each row and column of drinks is shown on the right and at the bottom. Can you work out how much each drink costs? Write the prices in the spaces below. One has been done for you.

ANSWERS

PAGE 4 -

PAGE 5 -
Callie spent $18, Cody spent $15.

PAGE 6 -

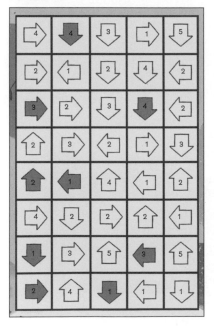

PAGE 7 -

PAGE 8 -

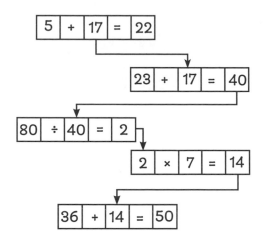

$$5 + 17 = 22$$

$$23 + 17 = 40$$

$$80 \div 40 = 2$$

$$2 \times 7 = 14$$

$$36 + 14 = 50$$

PAGE 9 -

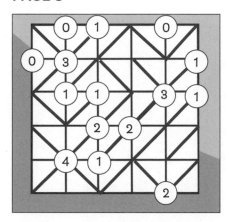

PAGE 10 - You need three swaps to create two groups of green dinosaurs and two groups of brown dinosaurs. Here is one way of doing it:

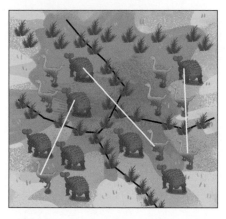

PAGE 11 - $32.46

PAGE 12 - Bear C

PAGE 13 -

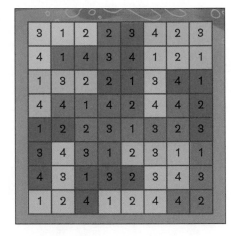

PAGE 14 -

8	3	1	6	5	7	2	9	4
9	5	6	2	8	4	1	7	3
2	4	7	3	1	9	6	8	5
7	2	8	4	9	6	5	3	1
4	1	5	8	3	2	9	6	7
6	9	3	5	7	1	4	2	8
3	6	9	1	4	8	7	5	2
5	7	4	9	2	3	8	1	6
1	8	2	7	6	5	3	4	9

PAGE 15 -

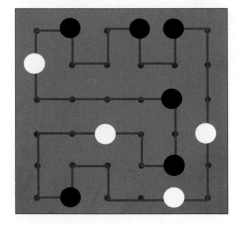

PAGE 16 - Archer 3 with 41

PAGE 17 -
A $21 + 29 = 50$
B $4 \times 12 = 48$
C $7 \times 7 = 49$
D $92 \div 2 = 46$
E $76 - 29 = 47$

PAGE 18 -
The meals cost $76.82, $80.24, $79.98 and $85.46

PAGE 19 - $8 \times 6 = 48$

PAGE 20 - $315 + 426 = 741$
$153 + 623 = 776$
$236 + 514 = 750$

PAGE 21 -

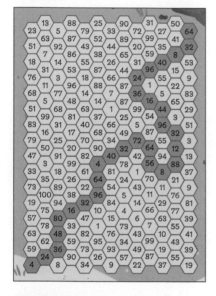

PAGE 22 -

= 4
= 3
= 7
= 8

PAGE 23 -

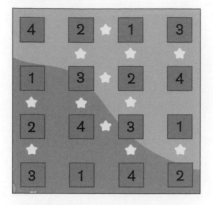

PAGE 24 -
Coffee was the most popular drink
Espresso = 107
Tea = 94
Milkshake = 43
Coffee = 114

PAGE 25 -

PAGE 26 -
1. 13 coins
2. No, she would need 3 more coins.
3. 6 chocolate broomsticks
4. 4 pairs of earrings

PAGE 27 -

X		X		0
2	X	3	2	
	1		X	2
1	2	2		X
X	2	X		1

PAGE 28 - Hippo E is the heaviest
A ½ of $9 = 4.5$
B $8 - 3.8 = 4.2$
C $2.2 \times 2 = 4.4$
D $16 \div 4 = 4$
E $2.7 + 1.9 = 4.6$
F $6.3 - 2.2 = 4.1$
G $8.6 \div 2 = 4.3$

PAGE 29 -
1. Harvey – 2 minutes 40 seconds
2. Harvey took 12 minutes and Hazel took 13 minutes 10 seconds, so Harvey was fastest
3. 3 minutes

PAGE 30 -
$9 \div 3 = 3$ (drum)
$8 \times 4 = 32$ (drum, violin)
$5 \times 9 = 45$ (French horn, tambourine)
$7 \times 6 = 42$ (French horn, violin)
$8 \div 2 = 4$ (French horn)

PAGE 31 -

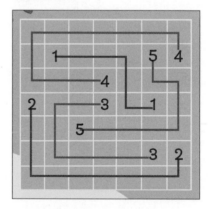

PAGE 32 -

PAGE 33 -

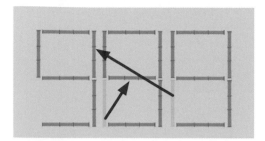

PAGE 34 -

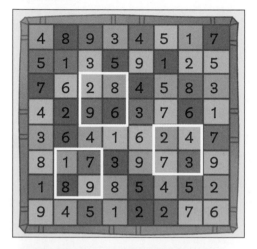

PAGE 35 -

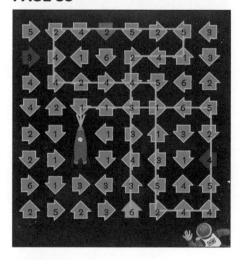

PAGE 36 - RED VELVET

PAGE 37 -

Puzzle A – F
Together, the letter and number in the
same square add up to the central total.
F = 6th, so 6 + 6 = 12

Puzzle B – S
The number is 2 back from the letter's
place in the alphabet. S = 19th

PAGE 38 - 35

PAGE 39 -

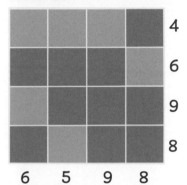

PAGE 40 -

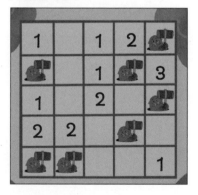

PAGE 41 - Pirate C has the
highest score
A: 2 x 6 + 4 = 16
B: 5 x 3 + 4 = 19
C: 4 x 4 + 5 = 21
D: 3 x 4 + 5 = 17

PAGE 42 -
28 + 9 = 37
47 - 22 = 25
2 x 12 = 24
36 ÷ 6 = 6

PAGE 43 - The 7 times table;
70 is missing

PAGE 44 -

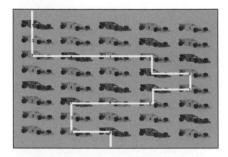

PAGE 45 -

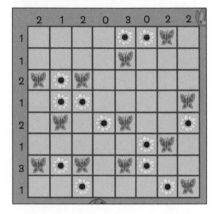

PAGE 46 -

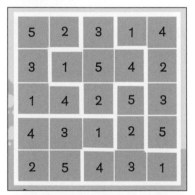

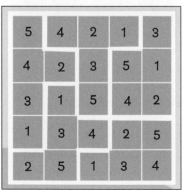

PAGE 47 -

PAGE 48 -

Turtle B travels the farthest:

A. 45 + 23 + 96 + 101 + 12 = 277
B. 28 + 139 + 56 + 72 + 5 = 300
C. 14 + 73 + 48 + 92 + 67 = 294

PAGE 49 -

C and E have the same total
   A. 19 + 25 + 7 + 14 = 65
   B. 10 + 13 + 28 + 19 = 70
   C. 29 + 17 + 6 + 14 = 66
   D. 31 + 8 + 15 + 17 = 71
   E. 12 + 6 + 33 + 15 = 66

PAGE 50 -

4	7	5	8	1	5	2	3	7	2
2	4	1	2	9	6	2	6	1	9
1	5	6	9	1	9	4	9	3	7
7	1	6	3	5	8	1	5	4	3
9	2	5	6	1	6	2	6	4	6
8	6	2	5	7	3	5	9	8	2
2	4	8	4	3	2	9	8	2	1
1	5	3	6	9	9	6	2	1	7
3	7	9	3	5	8	4	1	5	8
2	9	7	4	6	8	2	8	3	8
5	1	7	5	9	5	7	6	1	4
9	7	6	8	5	1	3	9	6	1
5	6	9	8	2	7	4	9	8	7
1	3	8	6	9	5	8	1	6	2
9	6	2	7	4	2	9	8	2	1

PAGE 51 -

3	2	6	1	4	5
5	1	2	3	6	4
4	5	1	2	3	6
6	3	4	5	2	1
1	6	3	4	5	2
2	4	5	6	1	3

PAGE 52 -

N = –
E = +
S = ×
W = ÷

PAGE 53 -

1. Tuesday and Thursday
2. There were more total riders on the weekend (190) than on weekdays (180)
3. €60
4. There were 60 more riders on Saturday than Tuesday

PAGE 54 -

0.5 × 66 = 3 × 11
21 × 2 = 6 × 7
100 ÷ 4 = 5 × 5
54 – 9 = 15 × 3
17 + 18 = 0.5 × 70

PAGE 55 -

 = 8   = 2

🍔 = 6   🍩 = 3

🍟 = 4   🍕 = 5

PAGE 56 -

55	+	28	= 83
÷		–	
11	×	12	= 132
= 5		= 16	

PAGE 57 -

1. Amy is 12
2. Bruno is 22. His dad is 22 years older, so now Bruno is 22, his dad is twice his age

PAGE 58 - 6279

PAGE 59 -

Puzzle A – E
The average of each opposing pair of letters = 13 eg A = 1 plus Y = 25; divided by 2 = 13. U = 21 so needs E = 5 to make the mathematics work

Puzzle B – L
Add the numbers in each column and substitute the total for the relevant letter of the alphabet. 3+3+1+5 = 12

PAGE 60 -

Cowboy B has ridden the farthest
A. 43 + 76 + 29 + 18 + 60 = 226
B. 15 + 82 + 47 + 36 + 51 = 231
C. 64 + 17 + 55 + 38 + 29 = 203

PAGE 61 -

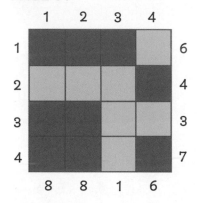

PAGE 62 - 7

Each row and diagonal adds up to 14 patches altogether.

PAGE 63 -

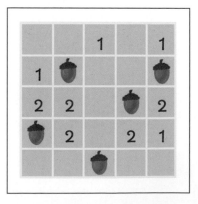

PAGE 64 -

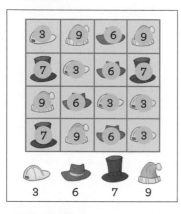

| 3rd | 2nd | 5th | 1st | 4th |

PAGE 65 -

3	9	6	9
7	3	6	7
9	6	3	3
7	9	6	3

3   6   7   9

PAGE 66 -

A. 9 times table
9 **18** 27 36 45 **54** 63 72 81 **90** 99 108
B. 11 times table
11 22 33 44 **55** 66 77 88 **99** 110 121 132
C. 4 times table
4 8 12 16 20 **24** 28 32 36 **40** 44 48
D. 7 times table
7 14 21 28 35 42 **49** 56 63 **70** 77 84
E. 12 times table
12 24 **36** 48 60 72 84 96 108 120 132 **144**

PAGE 67 -

PAGE 68 -

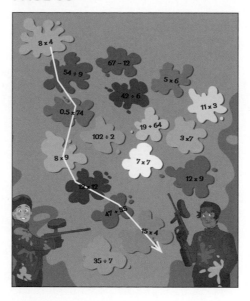

PAGE 69 -

The code is 5961.
117 x 5 = 585
481 – 18 = 463
150 x 12 = 1800
6 x 12 = 72
81 ÷ 3 = 27
8 x 7 = 56
1463 + 20 = 1483
11 x 11 = 121
842 ÷ 2 = 421
7 x 12 = 84
6 x 7 = 42
121 x 3 = 363
754 – 628 = 126

PAGE 70 -

4/5 or 0.4
30% or 1/3
2/3 or 3/4
3/4 or 70%
7/5 or 1.2

PAGE 71 - 94

PAGE 72 -

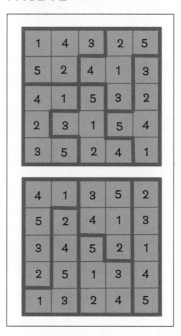

1	4	3	2	5
5	2	4	1	3
4	1	5	3	2
2	3	1	5	4
3	5	2	4	1

4	1	3	5	2
5	2	4	1	3
3	4	5	2	1
2	5	1	3	4
1	3	2	4	5

PAGE 73 -

3	2	3	5	4
2	4	1	4	1
5	2	4	2	5
3	5	1	3	1
5	1	3	4	2

PAGE 74 - 22 (cupcake)

PAGE 75 - E

PAGE 76 -
There should be 28 grapes in the final bunch (add 7; each bunch increases by 3, 4, 5, 6, and 7)

There should be 12 bananas in the final bunch (the sequence is +3 then -1 each time)

PAGE 77-

A = 8 C = 3
B = 9 D = 5

PAGE 78 -
Seven of the burgers are from the seven times table (14, 28, 35, 63, 49, 42, and 56)
They all contain cheese

PAGE 79 -

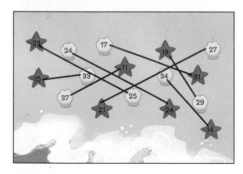

PAGE 80 -

6	3	2	4	5	1
1	5	4	2	3	6
2	6	5	3	1	4
4	1	3	5	6	2
5	2	6	1	4	3
3	4	1	6	2	5
1	5	4	2	3	6
6	3	2	4	5	1
4	1	3	5	6	2
2	6	5	3	1	4

PAGE 81 -
Group 2 adds up to the largest total (42)

PAGE 82 -

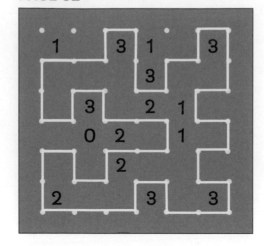

PAGE 83 - A is the smallest total.
A: 33 + 17 + 25 + 14 + 8 = 97
B: 51 + 20 + 5 + 16 + 11 = 103
C: 29 + 8 + 17 + 41 + 6 = 101
D: 46 + 27 + 18 + 4 + 10 = 105

PAGE 84 - SCRAMBLED

PAGE 85 - 77 – 13 = 64

PAGE 86 -
54 × 0.5 = 3 × 9
11 × 4 = 59 – 15
18 + 16 = 17 × 2
45 ÷ 3 = 30 ÷ 2
60 – 17 = 25 + 18

PAGE 87 - The campers in tent C will get wet
16 + 15 + 35 + 36 = 102

PAGE 88 - B = 168

PAGE 89 - 216

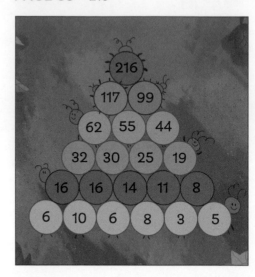

PAGE 90 -

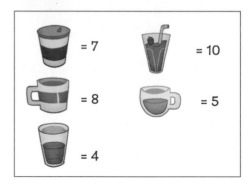

= 7
= 10
= 8
= 5
= 4